Kidvesting

The simple art of investing for kids and the family

Kidvesting

The simple art of investing for kids and the family

WRITTEN BY

Glenmore Wallace

Saskia Williams-Palmer

Stephen Taylor

Kidvesting: The simple art of investing for kids and the family

ISBN: 9781690159391

Copyright © Chosen Book Publishing, Glenmore Wallace, Saskia Williams-Palmer, Stephen Taylor

All rights reserved. No part of this publication may be reproduced, stored in a retrieval system or transmitted in any form or by any means, electronic, mechanical, photocopying, recording, or otherwise, without the prior permission of the publisher.

First published 2019

Cover Design done by Delroy McPherson

Book Interior Design done by Cross2Crown Designs

Edited by Monique Lynch

Printed in the United States of America

Business & Investing: Beginner's Investing

      Children: Money and Mathematics

10 9 8 7 6 5 // 4 3 2 1

PREFACE

The idea for this book came about shortly after I started working at an Investment company in 2013 and now 6 years later, the idea is finally a reality. Investing in the financial securities market is often considered to be an activity for the rich and the elite of society. I have noticed that this belief is prevalent in Jamaica based on my dealings with various levels of investors. In my experience I found that investments are done by mostly wealthy people, perhaps it is because people with few resources are instinctively afraid of taking risks. I tend to explain to them that life is about taking risks. Even deciding to cross the road involves a level of risk but we are comfortable with it because we are familiar with it, so we accept it.

In my observation persons tend to be very conservative when it comes to investing their money. A lack of knowledge about investment principles and concepts will lead to this predominant mindset. Nelson Mandela said, "Education is the most powerful weapon which you can use to change the world." "The power of education extends beyond the development of skills we need for economic success." This book was created to educate not only the Jamaican children but children all around the world about investing. If you desire to see success, you need to start from an early age and it all starts with education.

PREFACE 2

As a child growing up, my parents taught me the value of savings and putting away something for the future, but they never taught me anything about investments. I often say to myself that if I knew the things then that I know now I would be in a much better place, but everything in life happens for a reason. When I did my bachelor's degree and master's degree in Business Administration, I learnt the importance and value of investing. I also learnt the importance of working together as a group, which is why I enlisted the skills and expertise of two of my co-workers: Mrs. Saskia Williams-Palmer and Mr. Stephen Taylor.

I give thanks to Saskia and Stephen for joining me on this project, it took us 8 months to make this possible, but we did it guys! I know at times it seemed like this book was never going to be finished but with time, patience and a little reminder from each of my team members, *Kidvesting* is finally finished. I give a big thank you to Jamaica's two biggest Educational Institution, The University of Technology and The University of the West where I got both my degrees. I have learnt a lot and now it is my turn to pass on the knowledge to the future generation. I also want to thank my family for their support. To my beautiful wife Samantha Wallace, my younger brother Oraine Wallace, my mother and father, Sadie and Glendon Wallace thank you for your support. In Jamaica we say, "Big up yuh self!"

CONTENTS

	Preface	v
1	What is Investing?	1
2	Assets vs. Liabilities	20
3	Savings: The Piggy Bank	23
4	My Slice of the Pizza (Stocks)	33
5	The Simple Art of Budgeting	44
6	Bonds, Bills, Borrowing and Other Strange Words	48
7	Planning Ahead for your future	54
	About the Authors	57

CHAPTER ONE

What is Investing?

What would you do if you if you had one million dollars ($1,000,000.00)?

Would you buy all the toys you ever wanted? Would you buy your favorite flavors of ice cream and cake every day?

Would you buy a pony, bicycle or even a sports car?

I bet you would buy anything you want.

Well, if I had a million dollars, I would be a **smart kid** by buying a few things for entertainment and fun and invest most of the remaining money. Do you want to be a **smart kid**?

What is Investing?

> If you said YES to being a smart kid, then you will need to know 2 things:
> - What is an investment?
> - What is investing?

Investing is when you put money, time or any resource you have to use with the expectation of achieving a profit. People with properties/houses will allow others to stay in their homes and charge rent; this is a form of investing.

People who own cars will give it to someone who can drive and will carry passengers in it and charge a fee called fare; this is a form of investing because the car owners will benefit.

People will also lend their monies to other people, governments and companies who will intern give them interest; this is a form of investment

Smart kids will think of creative ways to put their resources (money & skills) to use to generate a profit.

Did you know that by spending your time studying your books, practicing to play a musical instrument or training for a sports competition, you are investing in your future? Anything that you can put to use to allow you to make an income can be considered investing.

Investing can take many forms, from you using your money to generate more money to a group of people coming together to pool their resources and then use it to make money. You can invest in several things like

1. Your own business
2. Stocks
3. Bonds
4. Real Estate
5. Mutual Funds or Unit Trust (pooled investment)

I am going to explain **investing** and **investments** by telling you a story about Roberto and his sister, Elaina who both live with their mother and father on the beautiful island of Jamaica.

Roberto is nine years old and he earns $250.00 from his dad each weekend for helping him with little errands for about two hours. Roberto saves each of those $250.00 in his piggy bank and at the end of each month, Roberto's father takes him to the bank.

At the bank, he puts all the money he saved up into a savings account where it will earn a very small amount of money and be safe.

Roberto loves airplanes and he would like to be a pilot when he becomes an adult but for now, he is saving all his $250.00 every week to purchase a radio-controlled model airplane to go to the park and fly it around with his friends. How cool is that!

Roberto has been saving for three months and after three more months of saving he will be able to afford the model airplane.

Is Roberto **saving** or **investing** his money?

What is Investing?

You got it right! He is **saving his money** which is similar to **investing** but still not quite investing.

Now let's meet Elaina who is another **smart kid.** She is Roberto's older sister who is sixteen years old and has a part time job working at the mall in a clothing store. Elaina has been working for a year and really loves working at the clothing store. She would like to go to college in two years to study and become a fashion designer. Elaina is paid $500.00 per hour and works 4 hours per day, 5 days per week and is paid weekly. She has been saving some of her money from her paycheck in a savings account for quite some time now and believes that it's time to try investing.

Elaina visits an Investment Bank every two weeks with her mom to put some of her savings and paycheck into a carefully selected investment. This investment will help her money to make more money and grow faster. **Her money will now be working for her.**

After two years the money Elaina placed in the investment bank account will possibly grow enough to help her pay for college.

Do you think that Elaina is **saving** for college or **investing** for college?

If you said **investing**, then you are a **smart kid** because she is investing her money for two years so that it can grow and help pay for college.

So, you see, Roberto has a **savings plan** for his remote-controlled model airplane while his sister, Elaina has an **investment plan** for going to college.

What is Investing?

Both Roberto and Elaina are **smart kids** because they pay themselves first using two methods: saving and investing. We are going to learn more about investments and investing in this chapter by comparing it to saving.

Investing and saving are almost the same, but both have their differences. A savings plan is when you put money aside for purchases that are going to happen in the future. We call those purchases **short-term goals**. Savings are generally safe and so they don't earn as much as investment because there is little to no risk involved.

Do you remember Roberto? He has a savings plan to make a **short-term purchase** of the model airplane in six months.

An investment or investment plan is when you put money aside in things like stocks, bonds, real estate or your personal business for the purpose of making more money to make purchases later in the future. We call those types of purchases **medium-term or long-term goals.**

Do you remember Elaina? Roberto's sister, she started an investment plan that will grow her money in two years to help pay for college. Two years isn't so, far right? Since college is not too far away it is called **a medium-term**

purchase. If it were more than two years away, it would be **a long-term purchase**.

Roberto's savings account at the bank also pays him money just like Elaina's investment but both accounts are different. Roberto is getting interest payments on his money; but it is still not much of an investment, usually investments earn more money.

You may now be wondering why Roberto doesn't put all his money in investments instead of savings if he can get more from money from investments. Well there is a little more to it than that, Investing usually involves risk whereas savings does not.

The risk we are talking about here is the chance of losing some or all the money you have invested. Risk can be managed by spreading your risk or a word call diversification. It basically means not putting all your money in the same investment or as grandma use to say, "don't put all your eggs in one basket."

What is Investing?

The money that Roberto puts in his savings account at the bank has no risk at all but when you invest your money like Elaina there is a risk of losing it. This is why you usually make more money in investments than in a savings account.

Elaina is a very **smart kid** because she started saving some of her money. When she had saved up enough money, Elaina's mom helped her to start investing by taking her to an **investment broker** and carefully selecting an investment for Elaina to invest a part of her savings and some of her pay.

Money Tips

Start **saving now** like Roberto and you will have enough money **to invest** when you are able to just like his big sister, Elaina.

LET'S DO A
DOUBLE-CHECK!

Okay **smart kids** let's make sure that you have this right.

Saving money is when you:

A. Put money aside to buy something later and there is no risk of losing your money.

B. Throw your money in the toilet.

C. Use money to buy something now.

If your answer was **A**. Then you are correct.

Saving money is when you put money aside to buy something later and there is no risk of losing your money. **Investing,** on the other hand, is when you want to use money to make more money. There is some risk with investing because there is no guarantee that you won't lose some of your money.

What is Investing?

The easiest way to understand investing is when you buy a skittles for $100.00 and sell it back for $150.00. You have gained 50% on your money or $50.00 on your hundred dollars. This is a form of **investing**, but it requires you doing actual work with your money. If you eat the skittles instead of selling it, then you just lost $100.00 but you gained the benefit of eating the skittles.

Another way people invest is to let other persons use their money for business, this is ultimately **stocks**. You have a share in the profits of other people because you have given them your money to do business with it.

An example is: If your sisters borrows $100.00 from you, buys a skittles, sells it for $150.00 and gives you back your $100.00 plus an additional $10.00, then you have gained $10.00 without doing anything. Your sister has also gained $40.00 by buying at a low price and selling it a higher price. Later down in the chapter we will give you more examples to better illustrate or show you what is investing.

CHAPTER TWO

Assets vs. Liabilities

In this chapter you will learn about assets and liabilities and the importance of making your money work for you.

As a **smart kid,** there are many things you can do with your money and the decisions you make with it will one day make you wealthy or poor. There are two things that everybody spends their money on: they are either **assets** or **liabilities**.

An **asset** is something that puts money in your pocket while a **liability** is something that takes money out of your pocket.

Some examples of assets are:

- a savings account,
- a popcorn machine that you own that you use to sell popcorn to your neighbors.
- a house that is rented and the tenant pays the rent, then that rental income goes to your pocket.

Assets vs. Liabilities

Some examples of liabilities are:

- cars which take money out of your pocket in order to maintain it.
- popcorn machine that you only eat from.
- house that is not being used for anything.

If you have more liabilities than assets that means you are spending more money faster than the amount of money coming into your pocket.

Table showing examples of Assets and Liabilities

ASSETS	LIABILITIES
Produces more money ▲	**Takes away money** ▼
Popcorn machine that you use to sell popcorn to friends and family	Popcorn machine that you only eat from
Car being used for taxi purpose	Car being used only for fun
House that you rent to people	House that is doing nothing

If you would like to be a **smart kid** and be able to take care of yourself, mommy and daddy and buy all the things you need, **you have to invest**.

 Money Tips

Please invest wisely. Purchase and develop **more assets** while having as **little liabilities** as possible.

22

CHAPTER THREE

Savings: The Piggy Bank

At an early age I learnt the value of savings and its importance in helping me achieve what I want.

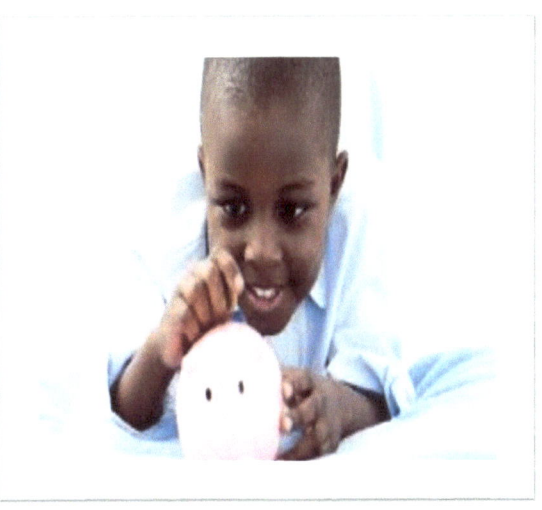

I grew up in a pretty average home, with both my parents working. My father was a soldier and my mother was an accountant.

They were making just enough money to provide me with all the essential needs a young boy could want. I was by no means lacking anything in life and this background taught me the importance of saving for what you would like to achieve in life.

My grandfathers were both farmers who earned a **living by planting seeds and watching them grow and then reaping the benefits of their hard work.**

Savings: The Piggy Bank

I gained a lot of knowledge from my parents and their parents, most importantly the value of hard work and planting a seed and watching it grow.

When we say savings, what exactly are we talking about? Investinganswers.com defines savings as the amount that is left after spending. In my opinion this not saving.

Saving is putting away a little of your

allowance or your lunch money. **It is setting aside a portion** of your

Christmas gift, money from grandparents, aunts and uncles for a rainy day, emergency or even for a toy.

Saving is an **intentional action**, not a random accident; it is something that is done first, before anything else is taken from the monies in your possession.

Let's say you visit your grandmother and she gives you $500.00 but you have a lot of things you would like to purchase like: candy, toys, games, clothes, shoes etc.

The first thing you should do is **take 10% of the money and put it in your piggy bank.**

What is 10% and How do I calculate it?
It sounds confusing! I don't want to do any Maths!
You're hurting my brain!
I just cannot be bothered right now!

If you are like this, then no need to fear. We are here to make your savings a whole lot easier. The calculation is simple and there are two ways to do it:

1. If there is a zero at the end of the amount, **take off one zero** and you will get **10%** of that amount.

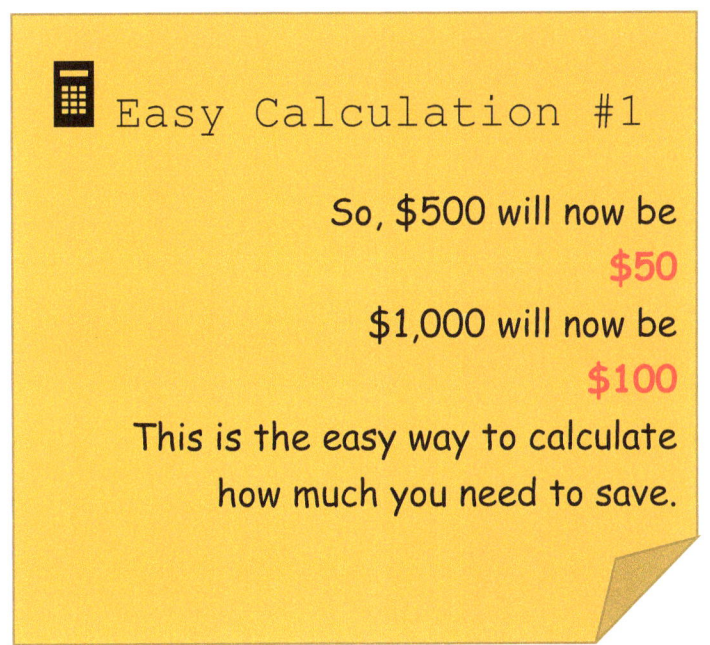

Easy Calculation #1

So, $500 will now be
$50
$1,000 will now be
$100
This is the easy way to calculate how much you need to save.

Savings: The Piggy Bank

2. The next way to do it is to **times/multiply the money by 0.1.**

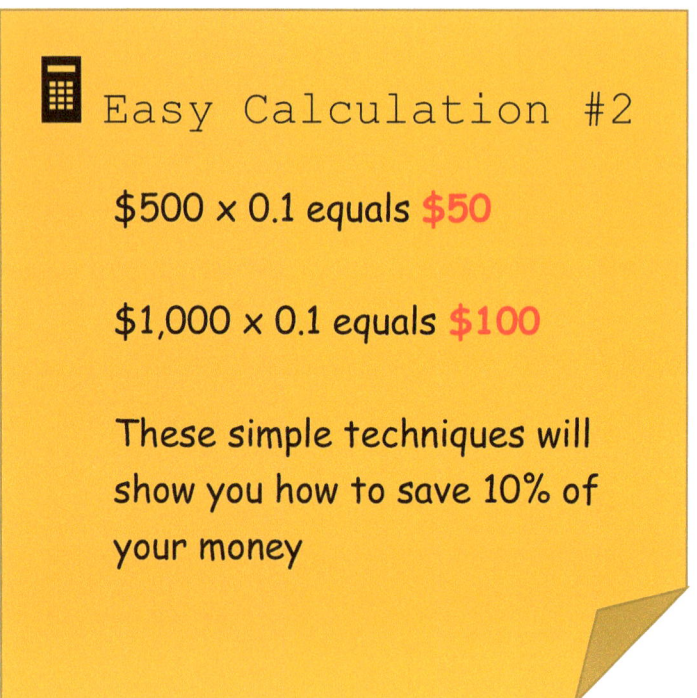

When I was 7, I received a blue piggy bank. It was really big and like most piggy banks, it had a little hole at the top for me to insert money. I was so happy when I got this gift because I always liked savings and this was an easy way to do it. This piggy was now my bank.

When you get older kids, your piggy bank will change to a real bank account. The bank account will be just like your piggy bank but instead of the money staying in your piggy bank, it will be earning interest.

Interest is a big word that means more money on your money. The bank will give you extra money just for keeping your money.

It is "muy importante" *(Spanish for very important)* that you **start to save as soon as you receive your first dollar**. I was able to buy several items while growing up without having to ask my parents for money.

I remember once seeing this blue and white bicycle in the window of a store that I always wanted and at the time I thought I would not be able to afford it. When I asked my parents for the money, they said they did not have it and that I can try saving for it.

In Jamaica we don't have a paper route like in the United States of America, where a child can make extra money by delivering or selling newspapers or even selling lemonade. So, I had to be smart. I started to save a portion of my lunch money and when I saved up to about $100.00, I was able to buy a big bag of candy or lollipop as we call them. This bag came with 24 lollipops and I sold each of those lollipops for 10 dollars each.

Savings: The Piggy Bank

I started to earn the money quicker for the bicycle and while I must admit, I did  help myself to a few of the lollipop; I was able to restrain myself long enough to be able to save up the $3,500.00 needed to buy that bicycle. Savings at that early age got me my bicycle, it got me candy and it got me that happiness knowing I worked for something and achieved it. I stopped selling candy shortly after, but can you imagine how much I would achieve had I continued.

Money Tips

To prepare for any emergency in life, you should save; to try and get anything in life that costs a lot of money, you should save. It is not hard to save, **ask mom or dad for a piggy bank and start saving today, you will thank me later**. You can even make savings fun by painting your piggy bank or asking mom and dad for a specific color. When you save and the piggy bank is full, you will see the joy that comes with saving.

CHAPTER FOUR

My Slice of the Pizza (stocks): Going with Mommy to the Stock Market

There once was a group of 5 friends: Shawn, Shane, Krishna, Romaine and Oraine. Shane was the eldest and Oraine was the youngest. Shawn had an idea for everyone to buy a large pizza and sell the slices and make more money. He asked all  his friends and all of them said no! What if it doesn't sell? What if we get hungry and eat the pizza? What if we can't find customers? What if? What if? What if?

Shawn eventually convinced Shane and Oraine to invest with him because he explained everything to them about where they will find customers and what would happen if the business failed. So, they knew the risks involved in this business venture.

Shawn, Shane and Oraine gave $50.00 each and they were able to buy the pizza for $150.00 and they cut the pizza in 12 slices.

My Slice of the Pizza

They sold each slice for $20.00 and they were able to sell all slices, they even sold 2 slices to Krishna  and Romaine. When they counted the money, they made $240.00 and a profit of $90.00. They divided the profits equally and this business venture allowed Shawn, Shane and Oraine to make 60% interest on their money. When Krishna and Romaine saw this, they were jealous and decided to do something like that for themselves. However, when they did it, no one bought the pizza and they had to eat the pizza and consider their business venture a loss.

Investing in stocks is similar to this story; you can make a profit or you can make a loss. Your success depends on how much information you have about the business you're investing in.

A **stock is like a slice of pizza,** the more stocks you have, the more slices of pizza you own. Stocks allow you to be a part owner in the business from which you purchased the stock. If you like candy, buy the stocks of the company that makes and sells candies; if you like toys, buy the stocks of the company that makes and sells toys and if you like games, buy the stocks of the company that makes and sells games.

Every time the company makes a profit, that will be your money making a profit as well. By deciding to delay or put off that desire for candy now, you can have a lot more candies in the future.

Stocks are the best performing assets you can have or own *(read chapter 2 and 6 for more details)*. While they are risky, they will give you the best return.

Do you make more money **buying and selling pizza** or **putting your money in a piggy bank?**

Buying pizza is the correct answer, but the risk involved in this is that you may lose some or all of your money.

> **My Slice of the Pizza**

Never invest all of your money. Invest some and put some in your piggy bank, that way you will have money should you need to do something quickly.

How exactly do stocks work?

You will ask mommy in your sweetest, nicest and most scrumptious voice, *"Mommy can you please take me to a broker or investment company and open a stock account so I can start buying stocks?"*

Mom and Dad will be so impressed that they will have to take you, Wink*. When you own stocks, you actually own a part of the company. Any business that the company partakes in, your money is being used to generate more money. If you should own 51% of the stocks on the market, you will now be the **majority shareholder** because you own most of the company shares.

When you get older you will hear the word **"equity"** which means **ownership** and you will hear **"security"** which means something used to show ownership in an investment.

In time all of these big terms will make sense, but for now, you just need to know that owning the stock is far better than buying the product.

If you like chocolate for example, you can buy stocks in The Hershey Company or Nestle or Rocky Mountain Chocolate Factory. If you live in Jamaica and you like ice-cream you could invest in Caribbean Creams Limited or Caribbean Flavours and Fragrances. If you like bun and cheese or cinnamon roll, you can invest in HoneyBun. These companies are listed on the stock market which makes it easier for you to purchase.

My Slice of the Pizza

How can I follow mommy to the stock market?

When you hear the word market, you think of either the supermarket or a farmer's market. A place where you  can go to buy banana, yam, tomato, pumpkin, bread, rice, bun and juice and this thinking is correct.

A **stock market** is similar because it is a place where you can buy stocks and sell stocks. We are living in modern times, so everything is online. You can go to Amazon and buy items online. Similarly, you can also go online to the Jamaica Stock Exchange or the New York Stock Exchange and be able to purchase and sell stocks once you have an account with a stockbroker.

If you are under the age of 18, you will need your parents to open the account with you in order to start you off on the right foot.

Most rich parents start to educate their children from early about the value of stocks. The fact that your parents have given you this book, means that they want you to have all the resources for success as the rich kids do. With this book, you will have all the basics you need to give you an edge in life.

💰 Money Tips

Plan for the future, save, budget and most importantly invest.

CHAPTER FIVE

The Simple Art of Budgeting

Budgeting is letting your money work for you. When you budget you create a plan on how to spend your money. You will know in advance the things you would like to spend your money on. This is important for smart kids because smart kids plan ahead. They plan for their future, they plan for their toys, they plan for their education and for everything they want in life.

How do we do this? We have to know how much comes in versus what goes out. These are known as **revenue and expenses.** What come in can be allowances from parents or family, and what goes out is anything you buy. If you see a new pair of shoes that you want to get, you first have to think: "how much money do I have?" if you don't have enough, then you know you will have to wait until you get more allowance so you can have enough. This is the simple art of **budgeting**, not spending more than you have. If you don't have it then you just won't be able to buy what you want.

The best way to budget is to know how much money you actually get first.

Once you know what you have, then you will know what you can afford to buy.

The Simple Art of Budgeting

You don't need to spend it all in one go though. You can actually put some away as savings for another day, so if you see something that you want at a later time then you will already have that money and you won't have to wait.

The key to saving is to not waste money. Buy what you need, not what you want. If you know you already have 3 pairs of shoes, ask yourself "do I need another pair?" "Or shall I save this for the roller skates I saw earlier in the month?" Maybe you don't need anything right now, and you can actually put all that money away for a rainy day. (This simply means for a day that you will actually need it.)

Try to save for yourself before you treat yourself. Look at it this way: the savings is still yours, but it will be used for something you actually need instead of want. Set different goals and save for different things. This way it's more meaningful and you will be delighted when you know that you have achieved this.

CHAPTER SIX

Bonds, Bills, Borrowing and Other Strange words

If a company wants to make a toy store, they need money to do this. If the cost to make the toy store is $1,000.00, then they would borrow the money from your mom and dad and they would agree to pay them an interest of $100.00 every year until they are ready to repay the $1,000.00. This is what a **bond is: it is a loan to a company or government**.

When you hear the word **interest, it basically means extra money that you receive for lending your money**. Banks pay interest, companies pay interest and government pays interest. If a company called SmartKid Limited needs money, then they can borrow it from the bank or from your mom and dad. When they borrow the money, they will pay interest, and this is how money is made. "Bills" is the group name for all the money your parents have to pay for your electricity use, water use, internet use, cable use and telephone use, just to name a few. "Bills" come in many sizes, there is really high bills and really low.

Bonds, Bills, Borrowing….

"Bills" will take money from your mom and dad so you should do everything you can to make sure mom and dad's bills stay very low. This is because when mom and dad spend a lot of money on bills, they have less to spend on you.

Borrowing is when you ask a friend, a family member or a company to give you something until you can give it back to them. If James wants to use a toy that his friend Veronica has, he can ask her to borrow it. This is the same for mom and dad. If they need money to help them pay for an item like a new car, they will need to borrow the money from somewhere like a bank or a family member.

When the bank lends them money, your mom and dad will have to repay it with interest or extra money. Borrowing is not always a bad thing, because mom and dad could be borrowing the money to buy a bus. Then, they will paint the bus and let it be used to offer tours around your country, parish, island or town to tourists and this can be used to make them money. When mom and dad make money, they can pay back the loan that they borrowed from the bank.

There are a lot of other investment related words that you will hear about. You can do some research online and test mom and dad on it.

These strange words will be known to you once you do your research and you will understand even more how to invest your money for the future.

Words like:

- Mutual funds
- Unit Trust
- Treasury Bills
- Cheque/ Check
- Certificate of Deposit
- Bank Note
- Initial Public Offering
- Dividends
- Coupon Payments
- Pension
- Mortgage

LET'S DO A
DOUBLE-CHECK!

Okay **smart kids** let's make sure that you have this right.

> Interest is earned when:
>
> **A.** You borrow money from the bank
> **B.** Your parents pay their bills on time
> **C.** You buy a car

If your answer was **A**. Then you are correct.

CHAPTER SEVEN

Planning Ahead for your future

The art of planning is simply getting your ducks in a row.

This means being prepared for a task or a goal to be completed, it helps with being organized. There is a famous saying that goes *'If you fail to plan, then you plan to fail'*.

Do you plan to fail?

OR

Will you be making that plan?

Consider a treasure map where **'X'** marks the spot.

'X' is the goal, this is the **final destination,** and this is where you want to reach.

How do we get to 'X'?

We follow the map, which will point us to different locations/clues that will help us get to 'X'/the goal. If you follow the wrong path, then it may take you longer to get to 'X' or you may get completely lost. The 'X' in this sense is whatever you want to achieve that beautiful bicycle, that cute doll, or that new outfit. Goals are not limited; they can be whatever your heart desires. All you need to do is put a plan in place on how you will achieve this.

As you get older goals and dreams will become bigger. They can be cars, houses or education, but once you follow a step by step plan you will achieve the same results. Just consider a bigger treasure map with the treasure being different things. The future is anything that hasn't happened yet. You can control what will happen in the next day, week, month or year. Set timelines and know when and how you will achieve what you set out to.

Take control of what you want your future to look like for you. This can save you so much stress and strain as you grow.

About the Authors

Glenmore Wallace is a Financial Advisor who lives in Kingston Jamaica. He has over 9 years' experience in the Insurance and Financial Industry. He has a bachelor's degree from the University of Technology in Jamaica and a MBA from the University of the West Indies Mona Campus. He has a proven track record of providing excellent financial advice to his client. He is the President of the Men's Ministry of his church and he has several certifications in supervisory management and financial analysis. He believes fully in education and knows the value it has on the children of tomorrow. This is the first book to be written by Mr. G. Wallace and it will not be his last.

Stephen Taylor is an Investment Advisor who lives in St. Catherine, Jamaica. He has a BSc in Management Studies from the University of the West Indies. He is someone who has vision; he is sincere about educating individuals about personal financing and improving their financial literacy. He works as a Financial Advisor and this platform allows him to carry out his dreams of educating clients and to help them achieve their goals. As a businessman, he believes strongly in entrepreneurship and in nation building. It is with this background that he decided, without hesitation, to partner with Glenmore and Saskia on this project. His desire is to improve Jamaica's financial literacy by starting with the future generation, the youths and the children.

 **Saskia Williams-Palmer** is an experienced Financial Advisor from the parish of Westmoreland, Jamaica. She has over 11 years' experience in the Banking Industry, working with two of the most prominent banks in Jamaica. She has a bachelor's degree in Business from the Northern Caribbean University located in the cool hills of Mandeville, Jamaica. She is also a certified Events / Wedding Planner.

She takes pride in assisting people to become financially aware and teaching them how to manage their money. She bases her excellence on her high customer service standards; this is key in making any business a successful one. She is a proud mother to a beautiful 7-year-old girl and wife to a self-employed businessman in St Elizabeth, Jamaica. She takes pride in this book and the time that was spent to have it published. It's a very good read for anyone interested in how to manage their money.

Thank you for reading 😊